6 Steps to Success in
Teaching with Technology

6 Steps to Success in Teaching with Technology

✦

A Guide to Using Technology in the Classroom

Lucas Kent

iUniverse, Inc.
New York Bloomington

6 Steps to Success in Teaching with Technology
A Guide to Using Technology in the Classroom

iUniverse books may be ordered through booksellers or by contacting:

iUniverse
1663 Liberty Drive
Bloomington, IN 47403
www.iuniverse.com
1-800-Authors (1-800-288-4677)

ISBN: 978-0-595-47937-5 (pbk)
ISBN: 978-0-595-48749-3 (cloth)

Printed in the United States of America

This Book is Sponsored By

Dedicated to all the great teachers in my life.

"Do not confine your children to your own learning, for they were born in another time."

—Hebrew proverb

Contents

Foreword

It is an honour and a pleasure to write the foreword to *6 Steps to Success in Teaching with Technology*, by Lucas Kent.

Lucas Kent is the son of two former students of mine, back in the days when films and an overhead projector were the cutting edge of technology. Both were outstanding academic students but even more importantly, school, community, and peer group leaders. It is only natural that Lucas is of that same calibre.

It has been said, "If students don't know you care, they won't care what you know." Any great teacher knows his students well and genuinely "cares" for them and their learning. When a high level of technical skill and the use of instructional technology are added to a base of caring, the opportunities are enhanced for all to realize their full potential.

6 Steps to Success in Teaching with Technology may be the beginning for some teachers, and enrichment for others, but it is important reading for all.

I join the board and staff of Burkevale in expressing pride and admiration for Lucas and his initiative and skill in producing a work that will benefit those not only in his own school but beyond.

Norm Mason
Director of Education (retired)

Acknowledgements

Everett L. Kent, for his insight, encouragement and ideas. He helped make *6 Steps to Success in Teaching with Technology* a reality.

Amy Kent, my wife and special education leader at Twin Lakes Secondary School in Orillia, Canada, for her constant support and contributions on assistive technology.

Norm Mason, Burkevale Protestant Separate School's Supervisory Officer. His wealth of educational experience as a teacher, principal, and director of education made him an ideal choice to write the foreword for this book.

Tim Mallon Burkevale's principal, for his front-line support and willingness to let me take technology into my classroom and our school.

Educational Computing Organization of Ontario (ECOO), for providing a wonderful forum for personal growth and constant interaction with my fellow teaching with technology teachers.

Inspiration Software, for allowing me to use their fantastic educational software to create the graphics found in this book.

Staff, students, and board members of Burkevale Protestant Separate School, for their patience as we introduced new technologies into their classrooms.

A Note from the Author

Thank you for purchasing *6 Steps to Success in Teaching with Technology*. I hope you find it helpful in learning how to adapt technology to your unique teaching style.

This book is as practical as I could make it. Let me explain. There are three things I am quite good at: trying new things, making mistakes, and learning from my mistakes. Teaching with technology has allowed me to do all these on a daily basis. Be assured, no matter what your skill level is, I was once there, whether it was making the machines work, understanding the software, or using both to teach.

Adapting to and using these new tools is rewarding for teachers and empowering for students. Children today are technologically savvy. They know how to communicate digitally and have been patiently waiting for the rest of us to join them.

Enjoy this book.

How to Use this Guide

This book is for teachers, written by a teacher who uses technology in the classroom every day. You can study each step separately or read the complete book in sequence.

- **6 Steps**—When planning the subjects to cover in this book, each item fit nicely into one of six steps. They are: *understanding the importance of technology in teaching, adapting to technology but also adapting the new tools to your style, planning for success, doing your homework before investing in hardware or software, implementing lessons effectively,* and *keeping up to date.*

- **My Classroom**—As a teacher I am always looking for practical examples to help me improve my teaching. Whenever possible, I added stories about my personal experiences teaching with technology.

- **Helpful Hints**—In many places, I added hints, tips, and recommendations to make implementing technology easier for you.

- **Highlighted Lists**—Lists help us learn. Whenever appropriate, I created concise lists to capture key words. I use these lists extensively in my seminar *Education Technology Made Simple.*

- **A Glossary of Teaching with Technology Terms**—When I use a term requiring a definition, it is in the glossary.

MrKent.Net

This book is not the only tool to help you transition into the world of Teaching with Technology. I have created a variety of online resources and seminars to help supplement this book.

- **MrKent.Net**—Our Web site (http://www.MrKent.Net) is a Teaching with Technology resource centre and a gateway to high-performance educational websites and teaching aids.

- **MrKent.Net News**—To keep readers up to date on Teaching with Technology, I provide a free online newsletter for educators throughout the world. I review current hardware, software, and educational websites, and I provide tips for teaching with technology.

- **Top Tech Picks**—The arrival of the Internet and the abundance of software, hardware, and thousands of websites created a dilemma for many first-time users. To assist, I created *MrKent.Net Top Tech Picks*, updated regularly on our website.

- **Teaching with Technology Made Simple**—I offer a seminar, *Teaching with Technology Made Simple*. For more information about our seminar or consulting services, contact lucaskent@MrKent.Net.

- **Help Us Help Others**—I am always looking for ways to improve this book, as well as my website, newsletter, and seminar. If you have suggestions, questions, observations, corrections, or quotes to share, contact lucaskent@MrKent.Net.

Introduction

Teaching is changing. Are you? Think for a moment of how far we have come in the last sixty years. My grandmothers attended one-room rural schools. These small buildings included a blackboard, chalk, erasers, a now-extinct disciplinary tool, books, a wood stove, and one teacher, usually female, doing her best to educate children of all ages. Can you imagine? Are there any statues for those heroic wonders of the past? A generation before that, my great grandparents had little formal education. My great grandmother, born in Sundridge, Ontario, in 1900, made it to grade three.

Two generations and only six decades later, their grandson the student received twenty years of formal English and French education, from dozens of specialized educators on three continents. Today, their grandson the teacher has many new resources, but the challenges continue. I have one class of ten-to eleven-year-olds, access to educational assistants, consultants, administrators, seminars for personal growth, and technological education tools to deliver information to my students in our small town of Penetanguishene, Ontario, from anywhere in the world.

Why is teaching still a challenge? Children are still children, with all the challenges of yesteryear—discipline, attentiveness, self-esteem, peer and parent pressure, and homework. Another significant challenge is that students today reside in a big global village, with big global problems. In this new world, information arrives at lightning speed from all corners of the earth. This high-speed digital highway influences most aspects of their society. Financial services, health care, the military, government services, and transportation are a few examples of where high-speed data collection, storage, and processing have forever changed the way we do business.

This technological tidal wave has now arrived at today's schoolhouse, revolutionizing how teachers teach and students learn. How is this happening? Computers, cell phones, digital whiteboards, student-response systems, projectors, the Internet, portable media players, software, and email are tools now available to front-line teachers and students.

xxii   6 Steps to Success in Teaching with Technology

What does today's technology allow us to do?

- Access information in various formats from anywhere at any time

- Translate words instantly from one language into another

- Enhance geography lessons with satellite images

- Tap into the world's webcams to examine our living planet or to interact with other classrooms

- Assess student knowledge using digital tools and adjust lessons accordingly

- At a single touch, access the world's news programs, newspapers, libraries, and museums

Preparing students to be citizens in this high-speed world is a significant undertaking. As a first step, educators must start teaching with the technology tools their students will use as future leaders and problem solvers.

6 Steps

To implement technology in classrooms, schools must prepare front-line teachers. *6 Steps to Success in Teaching with Technology* helps teachers learn about, adapt to, and embrace technology.

Step 1: Understand Why

Before an educator can begin to incorporate technology effectively into her classroom, she must be a believer. Step 1 outlines the benefits of incorporating technology into teaching.

Step 2: Adapt

Two adaptations must occur for success in teaching with technology. Teachers must adapt to technology, and technology must be adapted to teachers.

Step 3: Plan

Having a good plan is a key to success. Step 3 prepares teachers for the Teaching with Technology world by reviewing important planning questions.

Step 4: Do Your Homework

Before spending money, teachers need to understand technology options. Step 4 overviews the most popular hardware and software used in today's classrooms.

Step 5: Implement Effectively

Having the latest tools in your classroom may look impressive, but you must be able to use them to deliver quality lessons. Step 5 explains how to do this.

Step 6: Keep Up to Date

Technology changes daily. Managing this moving target is a challenge for busy teachers. Step 6 shows teachers how to stay on top of the latest changes in educational technology.

The Future

This text includes predictions on the future, suggestions for technology designed classrooms, and my confessional, "If I had to do it all over again."

Step 1:

UNDERSTAND WHY

"How can I trust your information when you're using such outdated technology?"

Every year, there is always a student who asks questions that go beyond the scope of our lessons. This student always wants to know the reasons behind what we are learning. They ask questions like, "Who invented Algebra?" or "Why do we need to know Newton's Laws of motion?" These students, like many of us, are trying to find meaning in what they are being asked to do.

Similarly, I am given many new programs to use in my classrooms; however, if I do not see the benefits they have for my class, they get used only a couple of times and end up collecting dust on the shelf.

As a teacher, you must understand why Teaching with Technology is important before using it. When you understand this, everything else makes sense. In the introduction, we examined how technology is changing the world around us. In this chapter, we will look at its importance to the school community.

In Understand Why we will try to answer the following questions, in order to illustrate the importance of Teaching with Technology.

1.   The teacher is part of an evolving virtual education community (VEC). What are its features? Who are its members? What tools do they use? How does a teacher fit in?

2.   Is the teaching world changing? What is changing and what is not changing?

3.   There are reasons for and against using technology. What are they?

4.   What are the benefits of technology in the classroom—for students, teachers, parents, and the school community?

THE VIRTUAL EDUCATION COMMUNITY

When I started teaching, the educational community for the most part included the teacher and the students. Today schools are evolving into *virtual education communities* (VEC) that have complex and dynamic relationships. Be aware of these communities and the role you play.

The Features of the VEC

Virtual educational communities have many features.

- Hardware and software make lessons more informative, dynamic, and interactive.

- Instant access to information through the World Wide Web.

- School calendars, homework details, school notes, field trip information, and upcoming events available securely online.

- Online tools enable the teacher to post, collect, and assess student work.

- Student creativity is expanded by utilizing various digital media.

- Student grades accessible and secured online.

- Club and team information, schedules, standings, awards, and results available online.

- Students, parents, and teachers can communicate digitally.

- Use of blogs and podcasts by teachers and students provide greater transparency within the educational community.

- Constant monitoring and upgrading provides better privacy and security.

The Members of the VEC

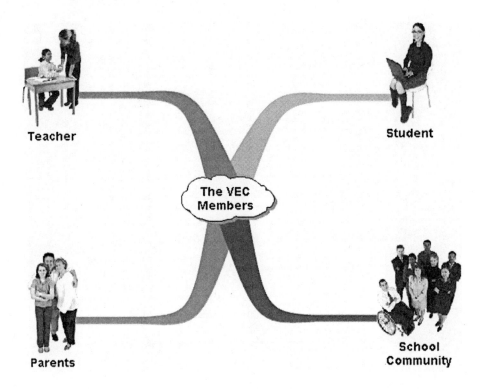

These members are all intricate players in the VEC and work together to improve teaching and learning.

- **Students** are the key members in the VEC. The community improves their learning.

- **Teachers** are the gatekeepers in the VEC. They integrate technology into teaching and help students use it to learn. Educational assistants help teachers keep the VEC running. They must also be technologically literate.

- **Parents** extend the VEC beyond school walls, encouraging online assignments, keeping up to date on grades and events, and communicating digitally with teachers.

- **School communities** drive the VEC to a new level and set standards that keep the virtual community safe, secure, and effective. Local community members and organizations connect the VEC to the rest of the world. Businesses, experts, and local organizations link with schools to better prepare students for the future.

The Tools of the Virtual Education Community

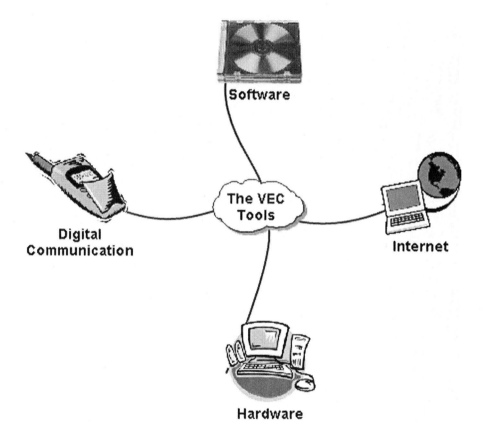

The use of these tools increases the facilitative role of the teacher, emphasizes self-learning for students, and increases the involvement of parents.

- **Hardware** in the VEC includes digital whiteboards, student-response systems, and school and home computers. These allow teachers to present powerful lessons, instantly assess student understanding, and extend learning beyond the classroom.

- **Software** in the VEC is used for lesson planning and delivery, student assessment, and digital learning.

- **Internet** allows rapid information access for all community members. Students and teachers access information worldwide through websites.

- **Digital communication** provides enhanced connectivity among all community members. The school's website is a giant billboard providing transparency of the educational community's operations.

The Teacher and the VEC

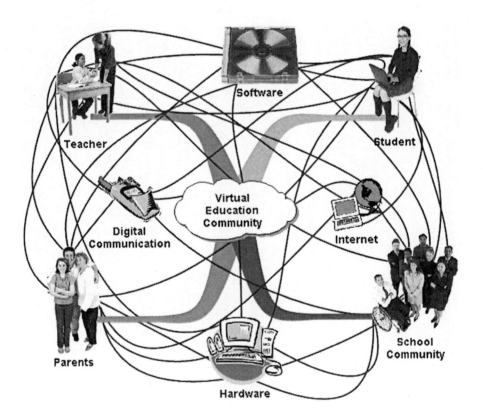

Does this look confusing? Are you wondering how you would be a part of this? Let's now look at the technology adapted teacher operating in her classroom.

A DAY IN THE LIFE OF A VEC TEACHER

It's Monday morning, another day and another fun week in the technology-supported classroom.

8:00 a.m.—Mrs. Apple (Psst! That's you!) walks into her classroom, quickly turns on her laptop, and reviews the daily news program and podcasts students will be watching and listening to. She then proceeds to check out the school's online community, where there are some announcements and where her students have been busy overnight finishing their online activities.

8:15 a.m.—She answers student questions online about an upcoming project and addresses concerns from a parent about her son's Math grades. The parent, traveling on business in the southern United States, has been keeping an eye on her son's progress in the school's password-protected online community.

8:30 a.m.—A journal, a Science quiz, and a French crossword were assigned for homework online. Mrs. Apple reviews marks and comments on the activities quickly and efficiently without shuffling a page. She smiles, noting the students' space glossary has grown to more than one hundred words. The morning news program will feature the return of the Space Shuttle, so this may elicit some additional space vocabulary. She reviews the latest entries and approves them to be posted on the school's online community.

8:45 a.m.—As the school day begins, a student who loves working with technology enters early to set up the classroom projector, digital whiteboard, and classroom computers. He tests the equipment and distributes the student-response systems to make sure they are ready for the teacher and the day's work. Meanwhile, Mrs. Apple loads several digital lessons and websites she will be using throughout the school day.

9:00 a.m.—The students enter and participate in the school's opening exercises, played over the school's multimedia system. The national anthem's words run across the bottom of the screen as pictures of the country's landscape appear on the digital whiteboard. Following the anthem, a short inspirational message is shown on the screen to give the students a positive start to the day.

9:30 a.m.—As class begins, a student reads the daily class blog she wrote the night before. The student summarized the previous day's events nicely and added some of her own unique humour.

10:00 a.m.—Next, the teacher plays a podcast created by two students about events taking place in their classroom, school, and community. The students included an interview with the principal to get her views on character education. The teacher is impressed with the quality of the podcast and the musical transitions added between each segment.

10:30 a.m.—Class continues with a ten-minute synopsis of world and national events delivered on screen, in a news-broadcast format appropriate for students. After a short discussion and activities related to the current events, the students prepare to find out more about their world from people their own age. The class links up with digital pen pals on the other side of the world, and a student-moderated discussion begins allowing both classes to ask questions that will help them with their upcoming geography projects.

11:00 a.m.—Once the online conference is complete, the students write a formal letter to their pen pal and send it via email. A few students attach animated movies created in computer class, while others send video of skits preformed in drama class.

11:30 a.m.—As it nears noon hour, excitement begins to mount as students prepare their questions for a special virtual guest—a real astronaut. Several classes across the continent link into a video conference with the astronaut to hear about the training she underwent and the experiments she performed while in space. Once they are inspired and informed by their newest hero, they continue to work on the space websites they have been creating.

12:00 p.m.—A few keen student Web designers decide to put their skills to the test and enter a youth Web design contest, sponsored by a multinational technology company. The students are so engrossed in the project that they spend lunch hour and weekends attempting to win the big prize.

1:00 p.m.—After lunch, Mrs. Apple has the students answer questions using electronic student-response systems in order to gauge whether the students have understood the previous day's lesson. After a quick scan of the quiz results on her laptop, she reloads a few pages from the previous day's lesson to give clarification.

2:00 p.m.—Now that Mrs. Apple is confident the class has a good grasp of yesterday's lesson, she introduces today's lesson, using video and interactive software. She constantly monitors their understanding using the student-response systems. Once the lesson is presented, students complete their assignments and the teacher works with a few students who need further clarification.

3:00 p.m.—At the end of the day, the class decides to add to Wikipedia. They have been updating information about the history of their town. One student has brought in an old history book belonging to his grandmother to help the class add new information.

3:30 p.m.—After the students leave for the day, Mrs. Apple sits down at her computer and analyzes data she has collected from student-response systems, online activities, and anecdotal records that she has added to her handheld device throughout the day. Mrs. Apple then uses this information to modify future lessons and transfers the assessment data to the interactive school website so parents and students can view results.

This is how the day and year continues in Mrs. Apple's classroom in this virtual education community. Interactive lessons, professional online presentations, conferences, hands-on activities, and digital assessments are used in interesting, efficient, and effective ways.

Are you wondering how your classroom can be transformed into this type of environment? It does not happen overnight, but it can become a reality if you make a commitment to add technology to your teaching on a consistent basis. Before you make this commitment, though, you need to understand why adding technology if beneficial to the entire educational community.

HAS TEACHING CHANGED?

Some things have changed dramatically in teaching, while others have stayed the same. Education has gone through various changes over the centuries—none greater than the one occurring now.

What Has Changed?

- Arrival of a virtual education community.

- Expansion of teacher tools available.

- Facilitator role of teachers.

- Increase in communication within the school community (i.e., between parents and teachers).

- Enhanced links to the outside world (i.e., digital pen pals).

- New skill levels required for both teachers and students (i.e., technological).

- Access to unlimited instant information (i.e., Google and Wikipedia).

These changes in education are truly revolutionary. Educators now have the digital tools to deliver lessons more effectively and efficiently, while students are not overwhelmed or intimidated by technology.

What Has Not Changed?

- Challenges of being a child

- Individual responsibilities of the student, parent, and teacher

- Need for well-trained, professional teachers

- Necessity of structured learning time

- Necessity of unstructured playtime

- Reassurance of safe and secure learning environment

- Importance of two-sided communication

Technology is not changing every aspect of teaching and learning. Remembering these basic educational truths will help teachers to bring together useful technology with good teaching.

THE CASE FOR AND AGAINST TEACHING WITH TECHNOLOGY

"For"

I have gone from a teaching style that used very limited technology to a style that incorporates technology into virtually every area of my teaching. I have seen first-hand the benefits that teaching with technology brings to the classroom.

- **There is instant access to enormous amounts of information.** My students are continuously asking me questions to which I simply do not have the answers. In the past, a teacher would try his best to give an answer or simply tell the student that he did not know. However, today, in a technology-supported classroom, a question like, "Mr. Kent, what does a fisher look like?" can be easily answered by taking a quick trip to Wikipedia, which will give my student the answer to their question and additional facts about the animal.

- **Teaching is fast and efficient.** When I began teaching, I found it hard to stay organized. However, once I started using technology, I have kept all my notes, lessons, reports, order forms, meetings, and grades organized efficiently on my laptop.

- **Feedback is superb.** Like many other teachers, I find grading to be an endless task. Now I upload all grades onto our password-protected grade book on our online community. Here, students and parents can check out their grades and my comments anytime.

- **Today's students speak "tech."** My students are always teaching me about technology. When the iPod first came onto the scene, one of my students taught me everything I needed to know about Apple's latest invention. Since then, I never hesitate to ask my students about the technology they are using. Tech blogs that review all the latest technological gizmos are another way to stay up to date on the technology students are using. For example, the aptly named gizmodo (http://gizmodo.com), and engadget (http://www.engadget.com) are just two of many great tech blogs.

- **The learner is engaged.** A reporter from a local newspaper came into our class one day to check out our technology. Instead of conducting a typical interview, she watched one of our lessons. When her article came out the following week, she continuously remarked at how enthused and engaged the students were throughout the lesson.

- **Students are prepared for a tech-based world.** When my students continue their education and head into the workplace, I am confident that I helped prepare them for our ever-changing tech-based world. I cannot teach them how to use every technology they will encounter. However, by exposing them to a variety of programs and technological tools, I am preparing them to adapt quickly and teach themselves how to use new technology.

- **Outside experts are available**. *National Geographic* has a live streaming video of the polar bears in Churchill, Manitoba. I regularly leave these live steaming videos on as students eat their lunch and snack. One day I received an email notifying me that the website was going to have polar bear experts answering students' questions live. As a class, we brainstormed questions and emailed them to *National Geographic*. The following afternoon, students watched excitedly as the experts travelled across the frozen tundra and answered their questions.

- **Technology is a window to discover the world.** The Internet is a portal, allowing students to see worlds previously inaccessible to them. One of my favourite class activities is to put a street cam up from a random city in the world. I then challenge students to move, zoom, and change camera angles to figure out where in the world they are looking at. Soon students are zooming in on street names, store signs, and newspaper boxes and working together to solve the problem.

- **It is fun to use.** During the day my students are constantly asking questions like, "Is there a BrainPop video about that?", "Can we used the student-response systems?" and "Can we watch *CNN Student News* today?" When my students ask to use technology to learn, they are telling me they enjoy learning that way.

"Against"

I have heard many concerns from people who resist adding technology to their teaching. Some of these excuses come from excellent teachers. I remind them that adding technology to their repertoires does not mean totally changing the way they teach, just that their teaching will become more current and efficient.

- **Technology is expensive**. When I describe my classroom to people in my seminars, I often see eyes roll and hear comments like, "It must be nice to have that kind of funding." True, many technologies are expensive, but with careful planning, budgeting, fund-raising, and even sponsorships, you will soon have your whole school fitted with useful technology. Our small publicly funded school started with one projector and now has digital whiteboards and other technological tools throughout the school.

- **It can be confusing and complex.** Technology can be confusing at times; however, most companies provide excellent support for their products. I have run into a few problems with our technology, and those I have had were solved by a quick visit to the company's website or a call to their technical departments.

- **There may not be support systems available**. As the amount of technology in our school began to grow, we decided to create a technology committee. The job of the committee is to address staff concerns and questions, to ensure that no one is overburdened with extra work, and to make recommendations about our school community's technology needs.

- **There are no support personnel**. I am not a computer specialist, and our school does not have an IT specialist on staff. Installing the digital whiteboards, setting up student-response systems, developing our school's online community, and maintaining our school's computer system are all done by full-time teachers. However, if complex problems arise or if staff feels overwhelmed, bringing in outside help should be considered.

- **Technology can be time consuming.** The initial set-up of new technology can be time consuming. However, once the main components are in place, using technology becomes part of the teacher's daily routine. In my class, technology allows me to spend less time organizing and setting up lessons and more time improving my teaching.

- **It is not an effective teaching method.** Technology is not the magic formula for student success. However, when technology is combined with good teaching practices, student enthusiasm, and achievement benefit.

- **It may take away from the teacher student relationship.** With the time I save preparing and setting up lessons, I am able to spend more time interacting with my students.

- **Teachers are not trained to use it.** Teacher training for Teaching with Technology is critically important and is one of the most common reasons for problems in implementation. It can be planned for and managed. Our school sets time aside during professional development days to help train staff on the latest technologies in our school.

- **Students will be distracted.** Students focus on lessons better when technology is involved. The lessons are more engaging and can be designed to appeal to the various learning styles.

- **The Internet has inappropriate adult content.** A major concern of many parents: the very adult nature of the Internet. Even a seemingly innocuous Google search can turn up some very child-unfriendly materials these days. This is why it is imperative that schools have up to date content-control software to keep students safe when working online.

- **The teacher can become automated.** I usually joke with teachers that soon robots will be taking our places. This is far from the truth as the teacher is needed more than ever because technology has created vast new ways to learn and teach.

- **Some students do not have computer access at home.** Teachers should not forget that some students may not have computers or internet access at home. As a teacher you should ensure that there is extra time during the school day for those students to complete assignments that require the computer or internet. Introducing students to your local library also gives them another means of accessing the digital world.

There are many excuses for not using technology in the classroom; however, all of them can be overcome by having the willingness and creativity to change the way we teach. I am not an accountant, teaching consultant, or politician. I am simply a front-line teacher experienced in the dynamics and interactions of educational technology in the classroom. Quite simply, technology in the classroom works! Everyone benefits.

20 BENEFITS OF TECHNOLOGY IN EDUCATION

As I continue to incorporate technology into my teaching practices, more and more benefits emerge. Before you take the Teaching with Technology plunge, understand and appreciate technology by looking at its benefits for students, teachers, parents, and the school community.

Students

1. **Concise and focused.** A lot of valuable time can be wasted during instructional time as the teacher hands out pages and writes on the board. Technology makes lessons more concise and focused and allows the teacher to move back and forth quickly throughout the lesson.

2. **Interactive and engaging.** With video, audio, interactive quizzes, and digital games, educators make lessons more dynamic and information rich.

3. **Relatable and reproducible.** When students see a teacher surfing the Net, or watch as he pulls out a digital gadget to help them learn, they relate to the lessons. These are familiar tools.

4. **Quick reviews.** In the past, if a student had a question, the teacher would rewrite information on the board or dig out overheads from her filing cabinet. Technology allows educators to review entire lessons from the past with a few simple clicks of a mouse.

5. **Instant feedback.** Students like to find out how they did on tests and assignments. Technology provides timely performance feedback. Digital student-response systems deliver instantaneous results with digital whiteboard quizzes and activities.

Teachers

6. **Lesson efficiency.** Teachers present clear and concise lessons in a fraction of the time. Time saving here increases one-on-one time with students.

7. **Decreased prep time.** Teachers spend a lot of time preparing handouts, flash cards, and activities. Technology allows you to spend more time improving lessons and assessing students rather than cutting, pasting, and photocopying.

8. **Instant assessment and feedback.** With student-response systems and online assignments, teachers assess all students and get instant feedback. In

the past, a teacher might assume every student understood the lesson until after a test. Response systems and online assessments help teachers evaluate each student's understanding before the lesson is completed.

9.   **Information and creativity**. Students have questions, and many of them are unexpected. Search engines unlock a world warehouse of data to quickly find the answer in word, picture, or video form.

10.   **Worldwide collaboration**. Teachers spend time and energy creating lessons that already exist. Technology makes it easy for educators to collaborate and share created lessons.

11.   **Improves communication**. Technology allows rapid communication with parents, students, and administrators any time of the day. The school becomes more efficient and keeps interested parents in touch with what is happening.

12.   **Assessment and organization.** Educators find it challenging to organize assignments, lessons, and assessments. Technology enables them to organize each efficiently.

Parents

13.   **Constant feedback**. Parents want to be informed. In the past, they waited until parent-teacher night or report card time to find out how their child was progressing. Now, with interactive school websites, parents can view grades and assignments any time.

14.   **Communication**. Instead of playing phone tag with a teacher or hoping notes make it to school, parents can use email to quickly communicate concerns or questions. On the flipside when teachers receive questions or concerns digitally from parents, they are able to address them once they have had time to consider their responses, rather than trying to give parents quick answers in the hallway or during a phone call between classes.

15.   **Visible curriculum**. Parents overview curriculum online to stay up to date with what their child is learning.

16.   **At-home learning.** Using home computers, parents can help extend their child's learning beyond the school walls.

School Community

17.   **Increased efficiency.** In business, technology is used to increase efficiency and save money. As schools integrate technology, they will see similar results.

18.   **Increased connectivity.** With frequent communication among administration, staff, parents, and students, the school community is better connected and develops stronger relationships.

19.   **Increased transparency.** Technology allows schools to constantly display what is happening in their community. Websites act as billboards for activities, from curriculum to special events.

20.   **Interactive and dynamic community.** The best schools are dynamic and interactive. Technology connects constituents, allowing direct input by stakeholders.

In this chapter, we've discussed how to build a successful foundation by understanding why Teaching with Technology is important. Taking this step means adjusting to a new way of teaching. It is not a one-time endeavour but continues throughout your career. Look each day for ways to increase your understanding of technology in education. In step 6, we discuss practical ideas on how to do this. First, let's look at step 2 and the role having the right attitude and adapting to change plays in implementing technology in the classroom.

Step 2:

ADAPT

"I think he's ready to start using the computer. He just said 'Google'!"

I am always amazed at how quickly students adapt to new technology. They experiment, share their experiences with each other, absorb new information, and incorporate the technology into their lives. As teachers, we can learn many lessons from our students about adaptation as we learn to teach with technology.

Change is difficult, especially when it never ends. Two teacher-driven changes must occur to implement technology in the classroom.

- Teachers must adapt to technology. This is not a passing fad and is now essential for twenty-first-century communication.

- Make technology fit your teaching style. Putting a personal stamp on each application is fundamental to success.

Here are some hints to help you better adapt technology to your teaching style.

1. **Be open minded.** Time will be the judge on how successful technology will be in the classroom. It works in my classroom, and I know it can work in yours. If you try to learn about teaching with technology with preconceived negative thoughts, I guarantee it will not work. Keep an open mind and continually look for ways for technology to assist you.

2. **Do not let jargon confuse you.** Why do we love short forms and jargon? In hospitals, it's ER, OR, meds, and IV. In the Teaching with Technology world, a growing body of terms can confuse someone trying to learn. Do not let any term, short form, or saying pass you by without first having it translated into words you understand. To assist you, there is a glossary at the back of this book.

3. **Ask for clarification.** Confused about technology or its application? Ask for clarification. Although for many it is a matter of having statements repeated, others may require detailed explanations, examples, or demonstrations.

4. **Be prepared for people like me, not knowing the answers.** Today's technology is developing so rapidly, those of us who work with it regularly may be unaware of a recent development, better website, unique application, or new invention.

5. **Be patient and find the answer yourself.** Search engines and online forums let you ask questions online, and someone somewhere will help you. Learning on your own is a great way to get answers and remember things.

6. **Do not be surprised if you are the first to think of something.** Be prepared to be the first to think of something. I encourage teachers to be creative when implementing technology. When first learning, you perceive with "new eyes," and this allows you to see what others cannot.

7. **Search for creative ways to apply technology.** One way to better adapt to technology is to test drive new tools in the classroom and at home. This excitement of hands-on discovery makes change enjoyable.

8. **So you understand. Think again!** Be prepared to learn it all again. Fast-paced change in the technology world keeps you humble. Someone somewhere is thinking of a better way. Creative new applications appear constantly.

9. **Never lose the "WOW!" factor.** Childhood was a time of saying "Wow!" to adventure and discovery. Our minds were like sponges learning new things. You have the chance to live this part of your childhood over. Keep your sense of discovery about technology—it really is quite amazing!

10. **Be a lifelong learner.** Step 6 in this book provides ideas for keeping up to date on the changes in technology. Get use to never ending learning when it comes to teaching with technology.

DO IT YOUR WAY!

Teachers use their unique talents and tools to give lessons in the best way possible. Socrates asked questions, others told stories and parables, while still others use comparisons or special projects. Each can be effective.

Adapt technology to fit your own teaching style. If several teachers were given a paintbrush, paints, and easel to teach an art lesson, each teacher's style and use of the tools would be different.

1. Know Your Style

Adapt technology to your personal style and strengths. Remember, Teaching with Technology is a matter of the tools adjusting to you, not the other way around!

Technology enhances existing skills. For example, if you are a teacher who uses games or contests to get a lesson across, there are a host of websites where you can find new teaching games for your students. If you use a great deal of student interaction, new tools can link with teachers and students in faraway classrooms.

Personally, I like to move quickly when I teach, giving students a lot of instruction and information in different formats, including verbal, auditory, visual, and hands-on instruction. I also believe in breaks. I use quick games and activities to help break up lessons and refocus students. I kept these things in mind as I incorporated technology into my classroom, and I now use slideshows, video, audio, interactive lessons, and digital activities when I teach.

Every time you incorporate new technology, ask and answer the following:

• How can this assist me in teaching my classes?

_____

_____

_____

• What current teaching techniques will be enhanced?

_____

_____

_____

• What new teaching techniques can I develop?

_____

_____

_____

• What information can I access and how can I deliver it to my students?

_____

_____

_____

• Can this tool help me better communicate with my class?

_____

_____

_____

2. Use Your Strengths

When adapting to teaching tools, be cognizant of strengths and weaknesses. For example, if you are slow to understand anything digital, make sure you have a patient teacher who encourages questions. If you are creative, make sure training allows hands-on exploration.

List three of your strengths and three areas for improvement.

Strengths

• _____

• _____

• _____

Areas for improvement

• _____

• _____

• _____

Managing your strengths and weaknesses will allow you to adapt to new technology quickly. You should not completely avoid your weak areas, but target them for improvement.

Improvement strategies

- _____
  _____
  _____

- _____
  _____
  _____

- _____
  _____
  _____

3. Know Your Audience

Technology is adaptable for various learning styles. In my years as an elementary teacher, I have noticed that different students learn better in different ways. Here are the main types of learners I notice daily.

Type of Learner	Characteristics	Preferred Traditional Activities	Preferred Technological Activities
Visual	Learn by reading and watching	Books, pictures, diagrams and watching others	Websites, videos, graphics and blogs
Auditory	Learn by listening and talking	Lectures, songs, stories, and reading aloud	Podcasts, videos, live experts and online discussion groups
Kinaesthetic	Learn by touching and doing	Hands on projects, building and experimenting	Digital whiteboards, educational software and video games

There is no perfect teaching method for all students. As you learn about each new technology tool, ask yourself these questions.

- How will this tool improve student communication? Are there potential challenges?

_____

_____

_____

_____

- How will it make parent communication better? Any challenges?

_____

_____

_____

_____

- Will this tool help with my school administration communication? Any challenges?

_____

_____

_____

_____

- How will this help with my school community communication? Any challenges?

_____

_____

_____

_____

- What new communications (students, parents, administrators, and other teachers) will arise from the effective use of this new tool?

_____

_____

_____

_____

4. One Step at a Time

Adapting technology to fit your style is an ongoing process. Do not try to do everything at once. Every journey begins with a single step. By simply reading this book, you are already on your way. Remember, our school started with a projector and a laptop, and today our classrooms are constantly and continually using technology.

Step 3:

PLAN

"There aren't any icons to click. It's a chalk board."

I am always stressing to my students to plan out their work. Whether it is answering a word problem, writing a speech or creating a Web page the most successful students begin with a good plan.

Want to be successful in teaching with technology? You need a plan. Where do we start?

- **Create the plan**—Visualize and write down the main objectives of your Teaching with Technology training.

- **Set specific goals**—From your objectives, set clear, detailed goals. Goals keep us focussed and motivate us. Continually achieving set goals builds confidence.

- **Maintain the plan**—Revisit the plan on a regular basis; set new goals and dates.

To help, here are twenty-five planning questions by category. Some help you make decisions, while others are for future consideration. A Teaching with Technology planning document is also available at MrKent.net.

25 KEY PLANNING QUESTIONS

Goal Setting

1. What are my long-term goals?

_____

_____

_____

2. In the next month, I want to be able to …

_____

_____

_____

3. In the next three months, I want to be able to …

_____

_____

_____

4. In six months, I want to be able to …

_____

_____

_____

5. By this time next year, I will …

_____

_____

_____

Policy and Guidelines

6. What are the Teaching with Technology policies and standards of our school?

_____

_____

_____

7. Who are the specific people I should contact regarding Teaching with Technology guidelines?

_____

_____

_____

Resources and Support

8. What support and resources are available?

- Personal training

- Financial aid

- Technology consultants

- Seminars to attend

- Organizational memberships

- Teaching with technology teachers

- Hardware or software

- _____

- _____

Hardware and Software

9. What technology tools will I need?

- Laptop

- Classroom computers

- Digital whiteboard

- Digital projector

- Student-response system

- Digital slate

- Digital camera

- Digital video camera

- Flash drive

- Printer

- Scanner

- _____

- _____

10. What is the cost and who will pay?

_____

_____

_____

11. Is there any manufacturer or distributor training?

_____

_____

_____

12. When would the items be available for purchase?

_____

_____

_____

13. Will they help me set up?

_____

_____

_____

14. What software do I need to get started, and are regular updates available?

_____

_____

_____

15. What is the cost?

_____

_____

_____

16. What training is required?

_____

_____

_____

Websites

17. Which websites should I be familiar with?

_____

_____

_____

Style and Skill

18. Given my teaching style, what should I consider regarding Teaching with Technology?

_____

_____

_____

19. What Teaching with Technology skills should I develop?

_____

_____

_____

20. What technical skills do I need to upgrade?

_____

_____

_____

21. What other self-development should I schedule?

_____

_____

_____

22. How and when will I develop lesson plans?

_____

_____

_____

Audience

23. What specific steps should I consider with my student audience?

_____

_____

_____

24. What specific steps should I consider for my parent audience?

_____

_____

_____

25. What specific steps should I consider for preparing my school administration?

_____

_____

_____

10 Tips for Taking Action

Many plans exist as only plans. Take action on your plan. Here are ten hints on how to do this:

1. **Have an action-oriented attitude.** I get pumped up about technology. When I first started this quest, I was excited at the possibilities that lay ahead. This type of attitude is contagious, and soon our principal and staff were just as enthusiastic about bringing technology into our school.

2. **Get started.** It's amazing how much you can do in a short amount of time. If someone told me in the beginning that in five short years our school would have digital whiteboards in every class, student-response systems, student laptop pods, and an interactive school website, I would have thought they were crazy.

3. **Have a coach or cheerleader to encourage you.** I have been fortunate to have many coaches and cheerleaders. My principal, board, staff, wife, and relatives all encouraged me along the way.

4. **Take one step at a time.** At first, I wanted everything to happen at once. Before my first year teaching I envisioned a classroom filled with technology. I was quickly brought back to reality when I found our school had only one projector and an old laptop. That is when I made the practical decision to try to add a couple of technological tools and skills to my teaching each year.

5. **Review, consider, and, if possible, answer the planning questions in detail.** When we began adding technology to our school, we quickly became overwhelmed with the possibilities. Our technology committee soon realized that we must make a detailed plan so that everyone was heading in the right direction.

6. **Record the actions you want to take.** Ideas for using technology in the classroom appear daily. I am constantly sending emails to my principal and throwing around ideas to teachers about new technologies for our school.

7. **Specify exact completion dates.** I set deadlines for accomplishing certain technology goals in my classroom. At the beginning of every year, I decide what technologies I want to learn or implement and set a reasonable timeline to achieve them.

8. **Set attainable goals.** Being practical helped me get to where I am today. When I first designed a website for my classroom, I chose a simple, easy-to-learn software program instead of the flashy, complex one I was tempted to use.

9. **Visit and update the action items weekly.** Our technology committee and principal are constantly revisiting the technological advances our school has made. This helps us make sure implementations are complete and forces us to review and learn from any mistakes we have made.

10. **Build in rewards for a job well done.** I have been fortunate to receive rewards for my work with education technology. I also make sure I take time to reward myself for completing a difficult task before taking on the next one.

Remember, great results come from an action-oriented plan. Take time to plan the successes you want for your classroom and school. Once you make a plan, you can begin "doing your homework" to make sure you have the best tools available.

Step 4:

DO YOUR HOMEWORK

"I hacked into the school computer and changed
all my grades. Then the school hacked into my
computer and deleted all my games!"

I do not believe in giving my students a lot of homework. In my opinion, the main time for school work is during the school day. Students should be spending their evenings and weekends bonding with family and pursuing leisure activities. However, when I do give homework, the most successful students are those that get it done and do a thorough job.

Make sure you do yours. Understand all the security implications, know the options you have in using technology, and have a solid grasp of the hardware, software, and websites available.

In step 4, we provide information on the following:

- Safety and security

- Classroom hardware

- Software for teaching

- Educational websites

SAFETY AND SECURITY

Safety and security is always a concern. There is no subject more serious. Protecting our youth and school community is paramount. The first homework assignment is to understand the security and confidentiality issues of Teaching with Technology. You can avoid serious problems by understanding the risks involved.

- **Security and privacy guidelines.** Know and adhere to all school security and privacy guidelines.

- **Confidentiality of information.** Information about students is confidential except to the individual involved and those with approved access. Data must be stored in secure designated places.

- **Student pictures and personal information.** Do not post pictures of students or any of their personal information on the Internet. Even if your school's secure website is password protected, continue to be vigilant when publishing personal information. If in doubt, review with your principal.

- **Internet security and protection**. Web filtering software prevents students from accessing or stumbling on inappropriate sites.

- **Email and messaging**. If a messaging system is built into your online education community, monitor student conversations. Have a software program or site administrator scan messages.

- **Educate students.** Educate students on personal technology responsibilities, online dangers, and Internet etiquette.

- **Blogs and podcasts**. Student blogs, podcasts, and websites can be accessed by others. Students must not post personal information.

- **Equipment security**. Technology equipment is expensive and sometimes the target of thieves. Make available published guidelines for equipment use and a plan for storing and securing.

- **Training of staff.** Ensure all new teachers, as well as users of the hardware and software, are trained on the school guidelines on security and privacy.

- **Software.** It can be frustrating and expensive when software is lost or goes missing. Keep all software accounted for and stored in one location. Do *not* under any circumstances use pirated software. It is illegal, it can be embarrassing for you, and it sends the wrong message to your students.

- **Professionalism.** Teachers should always be professional in their online correspondence with students and parents. Always keep copies of conversations between teachers and parents.

TEACHING WITH TECHNOLOGY HARDWARE

Educational technology is a blossoming global industry that is changing daily. There are thousands of products to consider when building a technological classroom. We do not recommend specific products in *6 Steps to Success in Teaching with Technology*. Product recommendations for our subscribers are located in our free newsletter, *MrKent.net News*, and on MrKent.net.

Teaching with Technology Hardware Checklist

- Teacher laptop

- Classroom computers

- Student laptops

- Laptop cart

- Digital projector

- Digital whiteboard

- Student-response system

- Digital slate

- Flash drive

- Digital camera

- Digital video camera

- Printer

- _____

- _____

Teacher Laptop

A portable computer is a staple tool for teachers. With reports, grading, attendance, evaluation, and lessons all going online, a portable computer facilitates
teaching and keeps you organized. Ask good questions when purchasing and
ensure it satisfies budget and teaching requirements. Select one that does what
you want it to do. Your portable laptop should be replaced every few years to
upgrade hardware so it can handle more and new applications.

Classroom Computers

Most schools have computer labs. However, these labs many not be available
when you need them. Additional classroom computers can help overcome this.
Even a few stations will give you more technological flexibility in your classroom.

Student Laptops

If space is a concern, another option is a pod of student laptops. These computers are securely stored in a portable cart available for quick student use. The pods can be used by small groups of students working on a project or by individual students who need the assistance of a laptop to complete work.

Digital Projectors

Digital projectors transfer digital lessons from your computer onto the digital whiteboard. When choosing a projector, consider the following:

1. **Classroom lighting.** The strength of a projector's brightness is measured in units called lumens. Projectors range between 650 and 6,000 lumens. The higher the lumens, the brighter the projector. Projectors less than 1,000 lumens are not ideal in a room with a lot of ambient light. If the projector is used for one hundred or more people, a projector of at least 3, 500 lumens is required.

2. **Projector bulbs.** Projector bulbs last about 2,000 hours. Have a replacement bulb handy. Check the projector bulb hour counter to see how much life is left. To make the bulb last, let the projector cool down before completely turning it off. Periodically clean the projector to remove dust.

3. **Electrical cords.** Wireless projectors are ideal for classroom situations. Unfortunately, they are still expensive and do not provide the high-picture quality you would get from a standard projector. Check with the store or manufacturer to make sure you have the proper cables to make the installation go smoothly. Measure how far you need cables to run and purchase any extra length needed.

4. **Mounting projectors.** If you are sharing projectors with other classes, you need a trolley to move the projector from room to room. If your projector remains in one room, mount it on the ceiling. Manufacturers offer projector mounts, and there are universal mounts as well. Make sure the projector is far enough away from the whiteboard and on the best angle for optimal performance. Digital whiteboard companies create boards with projector arms, eliminating the worry and hassle of mounting projectors.

5. **Safety and security.** Having expensive technological equipment in classrooms can be a concern. Projectors must be secured to prevent them from being damaged. Lock rooms or securely store projectors when you leave. There are special projector mounts with protective casings to provide extra safety and security.

6. **Service.** Projectors come with manufacture warranties; however, many stores and resellers offer additional ones. Additional warranties are usually unnecessary.

Digital Whiteboards

Digital whiteboards are an essential tool for the classroom. They act as an interactive slideshow, energizing students and enhancing lessons. Students are engaged as they interact with the board and perform tasks quicker. They write on the board with a digital pen, tablet, or finger, manipulating digital objects during lessons. Teachers can set up and reuse lessons and move back and forth between individual slides.

When our school first purchased a digital whiteboard, we purchased a stand. This allowed us to move the board around the school and adjust the height of the board. Eventually, we purchased more boards and mounted them on the walls of the classrooms, which saved space and time and gave teachers immediate access to the technology. However, make sure you account for the height of the students who will be using the board before you mount it. Digital whiteboard companies have also developed long digital pens that allow small student and teachers to reach the top of the boards.

When I first began using a digital whiteboard, I used it basically as an electronic blackboard. However, as I discovered the multitude of new teaching tools I had at my disposal, I began to really get the most out my digital whiteboard. Today, I use my digital whiteboard for practically every lesson and include video, audio, websites, interactive activities, and games whenever I can.

Types

1. **Rear-projection**. Whiteboards come in a range of prices and types. The first and most expensive type of digital whiteboard is the rear-projection board. No separate projector is required and users do not need to worry about creating a shadow.

2. **Front projection**. The most common digital whiteboard is the front-projection board. Shadows can be a problem especially if you stand in front. Students quickly adapt to using the board. Boards are durable and work well with a projector mounted on the ceiling or on a movable trolley.

3. **Short-throw projection**. These boards have projectors attached to the whiteboard. These projectors reduce the number of wires and the shadow effect by projecting the image from a short distance.

Several companies make digital whiteboards, and as the market becomes more competitive, prices will decrease. As with most technology, do not be surprised if the board you bought a year ago is dramatically cheaper the following year. Each type of digital whiteboard has its own special features, and they are constantly improving. Do your homework, and make sure you test drive them.

Student-response Systems

Student-response systems increase student participation. Designed like TV remotes, they record answers from students, who "vote" on multiple-choice questions during interactive lessons. Responses are anonymous or identified, depending on the situation. Responders are linked to software on the teacher's computer.

When choosing a system, ensure the devices will handle daily wear and tear. There are several systems on the market, and they are often designed to work with their respective digital whiteboard.

Digital Slates

In pioneer times, students used slate boards—which resembled mini handheld blackboards—to record answers, do calculations, practice spelling, etc. Today's digital slates are similar in some ways to their ancestors. Slates enable students to write on the digital whiteboard without walking to the front of the classroom. Digital slates get everyone involved, enhance lessons, and reduce downtime. They are especially helpful for students with mobility challenges. Digital whiteboard companies offer several types of slate. Choose one that is durable and easy for students to use.

Flash Drives

Even though most of our lives are stored on computers, we neglect to back up our files. Losing important data is quite high on the technology-frustration scale. Help yourself avoid these moments.

In the past, backing up files was time consuming and required numerous disks. Today, the flash drive backs up files quickly and efficiently. A flash drive is a small, portable data storage device that plugs into the USB port of a computer. Flash drives hold a considerable amount of data and are fast, reliable, and portable.

1. **Durability.** Choose one that suits your style and stands up to daily wear and tear.

2. **Size.** Find a drive to suit current and future needs. Prices increase with capacity.

3. **Compatibility.** Make sure the drive is compatible with your PC or Mac and comes with software that's easy to download from the Web.

4. **Write protect.** Ensure that the drive has write protect to avoid accidental erasure, and make sure the drive is password protected.

Additional Hardware for the Classroom

The same advice applies to digital cameras, digital video cameras, printers, and other devices. Ensure any tool is adaptable to existing technology and fits your plan.

10 Tips for Purchasing Classroom Hardware

1. Set standards around cost, usability, and quality.

2. Test the technology to make sure it meets your standards. I visited other schools that used the hardware and attended conferences where hardware companies were demonstrating their products.

3. Use hardware that makes you a better teacher. I believe the best way to decide on hardware for your classroom is to ask yourself, "Is this really going to help my teaching?"

4. Students must benefit from the hardware you select.

5. Have a specific budget and plan hardware purchases accordingly. When our school began installing technology into our classrooms, we were surprised at how the cost of peripherals—such as cords, stands, and ceiling mounts—added up.

6. You must be able to service and maintain the equipment. Having someone local service and maintain your hardware is important, as is choosing companies that provide efficient support.

7. Ensure all staff is fully trained. Our school uses professional development days and after-school hours to train teachers on new technology.

8. Make sure all hardware is installed properly. Many schools have their digital whiteboards installed twice because the installers are not teachers and do not take into account the size of the students or habits of the teacher during lessons.

9. If hardware is shared with other teachers, set up a schedule for use. When our school acquired our first whiteboard, I made sure to create a schedule that allowed others to try out the new technology.

10. Keep a hardware inventory and store the hardware to keep it safe and in good condition. This applies to daily, weekend, and long-term holidays.

TEACHING WITH TECHNOLOGY SOFTWARE

New software is being developed daily and making the right choices can be daunting and expensive. I follow these simple rules to help me simplify the process.

8 Hints for Purchasing Software

1. **Pirated software.** In our school, character education is very important and by never using pirated software, our school sets an example for students.

2. **"Free" educational software.** Do your homework on software. Programs can offer "free trials" that seem nice; however, if you begin to rely on the software you may end up paying a subscription. Other software programs may only give you their bare bones version, hoping you purchase a full version.

3. **Open source software**. Open source software are free programs created through the collaborative efforts of programmers from around the world. This software allows for people with programming experience to revise and change the programming code to suit individual needs. Many of today's popular software programs started as open source.

4. **New software**. I am constantly on the lookout for new and useful software to enhance my lessons. Some software is sent to the school while others I hear about from the Internet or other teachers. I never let a new program go by without considering its benefits for our school.

5. **Test drive.** Almost every software company provides free trial copies of their software. I have found that not all educational software is what it is cracked up to be, and testing the product is the only way to find out if it is worth the money.

6. **Licenses.** Our school always purchases enough licenses for our software. Most companies have discounts for multiple licence purchases.

7. **Keep organized.** I find that software CDs can quickly build up and can be overwhelming. At our school, we assign people to review and organize our software so that everyone is aware of what we have and can quickly access the programs.

8. **Updates.** A software program I use on a regular basis developed some glitches and became quite frustrating. After battling with the program for a year, I found out that I could have easily solved my problems by updating the software. Now I make sure to find out if the software we are purchasing includes regular updates and if any additional costs are involved.

Software Favourites

The Web is teeming with educational software. Here are some favourites.

- **Office programs.** Most schools have Microsoft Office programs or Corel WordPerfect. Microsoft Office remains the most popular office package. Base your choice on budget and features. If the budget is limited, use Open Office (http://www.openoffice.org), a free open-source software suite. It is compatible with all major office programs, such as Word and WordPerfect. You do not have to rely on Microsoft's programs when creating documents, presentations, and spreadsheets.

- **Worksheet creation.** The days of creating worksheets and tests by hand are long gone. There are worksheet creation websites and software available on the Web. Schoolhouse Technologies (http://www.schoolhousetech.com) is an example of worksheet-creation software. It allows you create personalized worksheets, maps, and tests in minutes.

- **Educational software.** There are thousands of educational software programs available for students to use. I choose programs that I can use during lessons and students can use on the computers. Programs like Understanding Math Plus (http://www.neufeldmath.com) are perfectly designed for teachers to use in class and students to work with on their own.

- **Textbook CD-ROMs.** Many textbooks have CD-ROMs so the teacher is able to project lessons onto whiteboards. Many of these CDs also allow teachers to modify test and worksheets, while others contain additional teaching tools, making them ideal for differentiated instruction.

- **Administration.** Educational-management software organizes student information, assessments, and reports cards. Not all of these programs are simple and easy to use. Be diligent and conduct extensive research when choosing a program.

WEB DESIGN

Many schools and institutions are developing their own online learning communities. These communities are part of the Web 2.0 trend of collaborative, social, and interactive websites. The sites have many features that benefit educators, students, and parents. The following are some of features of an online learning community.

- School calendars and upcoming events are available and easily updated by administrators.

- Classroom teachers post homework, project information, and field trip details.

- Parents and students access homework, project information, and school notes.

- Teachers securely make marks available online for individual students and their parents.

- Clubs and teams post information, schedules, and results.

- Students, parents, and teachers communicate with each other on classroom bulletin boards.

- Assignments are submitted and assessed electronically.

- Students and teachers can communicate via secured messaging and email services.

- Students participate in blogging and online discussion forums.

When I created our school's online learning community, I thought I might be the only one that would use it. However, as other teachers learned about the tools the website contained, they quickly became enthused and started incorporating the site into their own teaching.

8 Tips for Building an Online Learning Community

Course management systems are great for building online learning communities. Here are a few things to consider before beginning building an online learning community:

1. **Make choices.** Decide what features and you would like in the virtual community by browsing other online communities and consulting with your users.

2. **Prepare a budget.** Figure out how much you are willing to spend on your Web community. Using open source software such as Moodle (http://moodle.org) can help keep your costs low.

3. **Appoint a developer.** Have a computer-savvy staff member build your online community, or hire a company or consulting firm to build one for you.

4. **Prepare a site policy.** Prepare a site policy for all your Web community users. Make sure you address security and privacy issues.

5. **Appoint an administrator.** Appoint an administrator to maintain the Web community. The administrator can ensure the site runs smoothly, load staff and student information, run staff training, lead parent information nights, and maintain security.

6. **Staff training.** Train your staff to ensure the web community will be used effectively. This step is important, because many people will not use the community if they find it overwhelming.

7. **Information night.** Have an information night for parents and students to introduce your Web community. This will allow you to address questions and concerns in one night, rather than answering the same queries repeatedly throughout the year.

8. **Keep up the support.** Develop a good support system for your users. Use your administrator, staff, and students to build a network of support for all your users. Creating an FAQ page and a help forum are also great ways to ensure your community continues to run smoothly.

10 Things to Remember When Building a Class Website

If you simply want to create a classroom website, you do not have to be an expert Web designer. There are websites and software available to help. FrontPage, Dreamweaver, and iWeb are easy-to-learn programs that can help you create a more dynamic website.

1. **Check out other teachers' sites to get some ideas.** Before I started creating my class website, I scoured the Web for other classroom websites. Most of the ideas for my site came from other teachers' websites.

2. **Make a list of the features you want on your site.** I made a list of everything I wanted to include before I began creating my site. This gave me an overall idea of what type of site I needed to create from the start.

3. **Plan out your site on paper.** Sketching out all the Web page ideas before I started building the site helped me keep my site organized and easy to follow.

4. **Decide which website or type of software you will use.** I decided to go with Microsoft FrontPage for my website, because I had used it before and it was simple to use. Dreamweaver is another great Web creation software program that can handle more complicated designs.

5. **Keep the design simple.** My students and parents like our class website because it is simple to navigate and loads quickly.

6. **Choose a hosting company and decide on a website name.** Some schools provide Web space for their teachers. If not, there are many low cost hosting companies on the market that can help you get your website up and running quickly.

7. **Edit your website before publishing it to the web.** Spelling and grammar mistakes on your website can be embarrassing. I read over my pages a few times before I publish them online, and I even involve my students by offering rewards for mistakes that they find.

8. **Inform parents and students about the site and its features.** A classroom website is only effective if people use it. I use our class website daily in class and remind parents about it in every monthly newsletter.

9. **Do not publish any photos or last names of students.** I get permission from parents to publish student work on our website, but I never publish photos or last names of students.

10. **Update the site regularly to give people a reason to visit.** If students and parents do not have reasons to visit the site regularly, it will quickly become

useless. I add spelling, homework, and weekly trivia games to entice students to keep on using the site.

A class website helps you communicate better with students and parents. Do not try to do everything at once. Begin by adding simple features, such as homework information, a class calendar, and links to useful websites. Once you get your site up and running, you can add advanced features, such as daily blogs, an audio cast, classroom trivia games, and class notes. The key is to start simple and build in small steps. In a few years, you will have an amazing classroom website.

ASSISTIVE TECHNOLOGY

Educational technology has helped students with special needs for decades. Students suffering from physical and intellectual disabilities use technology to complete tasks and work on assignments. In the past, the knowledge, availability, and cost of these tools enabled only a small group of high-needs students to benefit. Today, they are more available, and educators realize these tools can enhance a struggling student's understanding of a lesson.

8 Benefits of Assistive Technology

The benefits of using assistive technology in the classroom far outweigh the disadvantages of cost, set-up, and maintenance.

1. **Increased independence and ownership.** I noticed that students who struggle need a lot of help from parents, educational assistants, and teachers to get their work done. However, when I gave them the appropriate assistive-technology tools, they were able to complete most of the work on their own and were quick to let me know they did it by themselves.

2. **Decreased frustration.** When I assigned a project or an assignment, my students were enthusiastic and eager to get started. Not long into the work period, some students began to lose interest, because it was taking them so long to read or write what they wanted. Giving them the appropriate assistive-technology tools removed that frustration and allowed them to experience the same learning as other students.

3. **Improved quality of work.** Many of my students have great ideas and the ability to do excellent work. However, their work often suffers because they struggle with spelling, writing, reading, or all of these skills. Assistive technology allows students that struggle to hand in quality work.

4. **Increased pride in work.** My students who use assistive technology are more willing to display their work, because it looks the same as other students' work.

5. **Enhanced student confidence.** My students who use assistive technology do not have a hopeless look in their eyes when work is assigned. They are confident that they can complete the work, because they have the tools at hand to assist them.

6. **More positive attitude towards school.** During interview time, parents always remark on how their child is more enthusiastic about school because of the technology they are using to do their work.

7. **Students more engaged.** When students know they can do something, they listen better and are more eager to follow instructions.

8. **Easy to adapt.** When I prepare my lessons, I always keep in mind students that may use assistive technology. There may be little changes I can make in the assignment that will allow them to complete their work with ease.

4 Useful Assistive Technology Tools

Reading technology

These programs scan text and read it back to students. They are essential for students with reading comprehension difficulties. Kurzweil and Premier are two examples of reading technology.

Speech-to-text software

This software translates student speech into written text. It is beneficial to students who struggle with the mechanics of writing, spelling, or putting thoughts onto paper. Dragon Naturally Speaking and SpeakQ are two examples of the speech recognition programs available.

Word prediction software

Word prediction software makes writing easier by predicting words, reading words aloud, and spell-checking text. These programs work alongside standard word processing software. Co-Writer and WordQ are two examples of word prediction programs.

Concept mapping software

Visual learning tools help students organize and prioritize information visually. Students create visual maps, outlines, diagrams, and more to help them understand lessons and complete assignments. Inspiration and SMART Ideas are two of the concept mapping programs available.

Choosing Assistive Technology

Ask these questions when choosing assistive technology.

• How much set-up is required?

_____

_____

_____

• What type of maintenance is required?

_____

_____

_____

• Is it engaging and user friendly?

_____

_____

_____

• How much assistance will be required?

_____

_____

_____

The best assistive technologies are simple and useful. Software that requires too much set-up and training is quickly put on a shelf to collect dust. Be sure to ask for trial copies of the software and let your staff and students test it out before making a major purchase.

Having the right tools for the job is important when teaching with technology. In step 5, we focus on implementing these tools effectively in your classroom.

Step 5:

IMPLEMENT EFFECTIVELY

"You have to solve this problem by yourself. You can't call tech support."

The key to delivering an effective lesson with technology is making sure all the support is in place and that you are at your best at the point of delivery. You can have the greatest plans in the world, as well as the finest hardware, software, training and technology talent available, but all these factors must come together before you can deliver high-quality lessons to students.

E-TEACHING OPTIONS

A good plan is one of the keys to delivering a successful lesson. You have many choices on how to deliver a lesson. Creatively using the digital resources available will ensure dynamic, interactive, and information-rich lessons. Understand the hardware, software, and website options available to you. Select combinations that bring your unique skills and delivery method together in the most effective way possible. Here are some examples.

Digital Whiteboard Lessons

Digital whiteboard lessons are beneficial for teachers and students. However, creating them adds extra work to an educator's life. Digital whiteboard companies have created great software programs and online resource centers to provide educators with the tools they need to create great interactive lessons.

The learning curve is about a year until the teacher begins using digital whiteboards effectively. Most teachers use their digital whiteboard as a regular whiteboard in the beginning. I found that the more I was exposed to quality interactive whiteboard lessons in my first year, the better each digital whiteboard lesson became.

Digital Tests and Activities

Creating digital activities and assessments can be difficult on your own. There are many software programs that can help. Hot Potatoes Suite (http://hot-pot.uvic.ca) is one of the quality lesson-creation programs. Developed by the University of Victoria in British Columbia, the software allows educators to create interactive multiple-choice, short-answer, crossword, matching, and cloze exercises. Hot Potatoes is free for those working in non-profit educational institutions. The quizzes are simple to create, they are easy for students to complete, and they save teachers time.

I create a few of these activities for my students every week. I use them primarily as review activities for students to do at home or when we are in the computer lab. These activities are uploaded onto our online community, and I usually give students several tries to complete them to build confidence and ensure they review the material as much as possible.

Podcasting

A podcast is an audio file uploaded to the Internet where others can download and listen to on their personal media player or computer. Professional podcasts are a wonderful e-option to enhance lessons. They are available online for almost every subject. Websites like The Education Podcasting Network (http://www.epnweb.org) bring together podcasts for teachers to use in their lessons.

Teachers can create their own podcast lessons, which students can review at their own pace. This allows students to listen to lessons or review for tests as they walk to school, while on a trip with their family, or before they go to bed. While these audio lessons should not replace traditional studying methods, they can be another useful learning tool for students.

Teachers and students can create podcasts with podcasting software. These programs allow users to record, cut, copy, mix, splice, and alter pitch. Mac users have access to a rich program called Garage Band, which allows users to create and download podcasts. PC users can download Audacity (http://audacity.souceforge.net), a free software program that allows them to record and edit sounds. This open-source software is easy to use and works on most operating systems.

Every few weeks, I assign two students to create a podcast about our class, school, and community. Even though I ask students to work on the podcast during recess, I always get plenty of volunteers. Once they are chosen, the two students write out a three-minute script and practice working with the software and microphone. When they feel confident, they create, edit, and upload their podcast. My class is always eager to hear the latest podcast, and it is a great boost to the confidence of the students who create it.

Blogging

Blogs (online journals) can be used to improve writing, reading, and media literacy skills. Online programs like WordPress (http://wordpress.com) and Blogger (https://www.blogger.com) make it simple for teachers and students to create blogs.

Blogging is a great way to improve literacy. For example, starting a blog during a novel study is a great way to create a forum where students can discuss and respond to different questions about the book. Every day I assign a student to be our classroom blogger. The student is responsible for taking notes throughout the day and writing a blog about our day. This activity not only improves their writing and recount skills, but it allows parents to read firsthand what is taking place in our class.

Wikis

Wikis are collections of web pages that allow anyone to modify, add or remove content. Wikipedia the online encyclopedia, is the most well known wiki. These collaborative websites are ideal for class and group projects. Students will learn how to work together to collect, organize and display information. WetPaint, WikiPB and Wikispaces are just some of the places where you can create a wiki.

WebQuests

The Internet has thousands of WebQuests created by educators. These are lessons that require students to use the World Wide Web to learn about a topic. Teachers can use WebQuests to replace the traditional read-the-chapter-and-answer the-questions-type assignment. They are also a good way to focus students on specific websites to prevent them from wasting time searching the Internet for information. WebQuest.Org (https://www.webquest.org) is a great place to start if you are looking for a specific WebQuest or are interested in creating your own.

Digital Cameras

Using a digital camera and video recorders can enhance lessons and projects. Digital photos can be taken of student work and posted online. This lets students share their work with relatives and friends, providing a tremendous boost to their self-esteem.

Digital cameras and video recorders can also be used by students for projects and presentations. Many students become enthused and more creative when working with these tools. During drama classes, I allow a group to record their play with our video recorder to expose them to using media.

Educational Websites

Simply incorporating high-quality websites into lessons can have a tremendous impact on learning. Students are exposed to current and dynamic information, accessible both at school and home. In appendix A and our on our MrKent.net website, we list current top websites for teachers, students, and parents.

Educational Videos

Online or from the library, short educational videos are another way to enhance lessons. Sites such as BrainPOP (http://www.brainpop.com) contain hundreds of educational videos on numerous subjects. I use these videos to introduce or review a lesson. The key to using educational videos is to keep them short and not to overuse them.

Educational Software

There is a great deal of educational software on the market, and new programs are arriving daily. Teachers must be familiar with the educational software that students use. Finding the best software can be a daunting task. To help, we review some of the top educational software in our newsletter, *MrKent.net News*, and on MrKent.net.

Computer Games

Using computer games to reinforce a concept or lesson is a great way to learn and have fun. These games can be found online and purchased as software.

For example, when I teach estimating angles, I use a game called Banana Hunt. By the end of the week, students are playing the game every chance they get, trying to beat the class record and sharpening their math skills along the way.

EFFECTIVE DELIVERY

Delivering these e-teaching options effectively is crucial. Relying on one too much or not using another to its full potential can limit student learning. Here are three things I always remember to do when presenting lessons to students.

Add Variety

Adding variety to lessons keeps students engaged. Draw information from several resources when teaching students without overwhelming them.

Take Breaks

Even adults have a hard time focusing on a task for an extended period. Plan breaks to refresh students and keep them focussed. I use exercises, games, songs, and stories to break up lesson time and refocus students.

Encourage Student Involvement

Educators are hesitant to let students use technology tools in the classroom or forget to plan student involvement. Some fear students may damage the technology tools or slow down the flow of the lesson. On the contrary, the use of technology by students reduces the time a teacher spends talking in front of the class and enhances student learning.

5 Ways to Increase Student Involvement

1. **Build technology into learning stations.** When I design lessons in stations, I make sure to include stations that involve technology. Setting up activities on the classroom computers, laptops, and digital whiteboard is a great way to get students using the classroom technology.

2. **Provide students easy access to technology tools.** Our classroom computers, laptops, and digital whiteboard are always easily accessible to students. I also assign students to be in charge of certain technologies to give them a sense of ownership and pride.

3. **Build in free time for students to experiment and explore technology.** I frequently leave the digital whiteboard and computers on during snack and lunchtime. During this time, students explore new programs or do their favourite activities.

4. **Strategically group and partner students to facilitate the use of technology.** Some students can become frustrated quickly with technology. I make sure that I group these types of students with students who are confident using technology. This ensures that the activity goes smoothly and keeps frustrations low.

5. **Assign projects requiring technology.** I make sure that all the projects I assign require some type of technology use—whether it is creating a brochure, website, video, or podcast, or simply using a word processor.

LISTEN, WATCH, AND RECORD

Student-response systems and online activities increase and improve assessment in your classroom. Used with traditional assessment methods, these new tools provide the educator with a deeper understanding of their students. The regular use of laptops and handheld devices allows you to input daily observations immediately into an educational management program.

4 Useful Assessment Tools

1. **Traditional assessment methods.** I still use traditional assessment tools in my classroom. Rubrics, anecdotal notes, portfolios, interviews, quizzes, and tests are all useful tools to evaluate your students and your teaching.

2. **Student-response systems.** I use the student-response systems at the end of lessons to gauge whether students have grasped the concepts. I do not add many questions; otherwise, students feel as if I am testing them and may become anxious about the lesson.

3. **Online activities.** I try to give students a few online activities each week. These activities may be matching activities, multiple-choice quizzes, crosswords, journals, or cloze activities to help them review the concepts we learned in class. The best part of these assessments is that many of them are marked automatically for the teacher.

4. **Laptops and handheld devices.** Whether I use traditional assessment methods, student-response systems, or online activities, I make sure I store them on my laptop. When it comes to report card time, I have everything recorded and categorized in one place.

BUILD IN THE FUN FACTOR

Make learning fun for students. Do the same for yourself. Attitudes have a significant impact on success. Having fun and learning at the same time is a wonderful experience.

5 Ways to Build in Fun

1. **Cultivate a positive fun attitude.** When learning about technology ask these questions:

   • How can I make this learning experience interesting and enjoyable?

   • What neat things will I be able to do with this new information and skills?

2. **Use engaging words like "discover," "explore," "invent," and "create."** Positive affirmations produce positive results. The words we think and say can change our attitudes and actions. This is especially true when learning how to use technology. It can be frustrating when machines do not respond, software becomes confusing, and students know more than you. Think positive!

3. **Never lose the WOW! experience.** Somewhere along the line, we misplace the wonder of childhood discovery. When young, every day brought excitement. Resurrect this feeling and build in the "wow" factor into your learning. Remember, with technology, you have access to the Louvre in Paris, a webcam in Africa, or even an astronaut in space. These are reasons to get excited.

4. **Involve others in your journey of discovery.** One of the best ways to have fun is to involve others in your voyage of discovery. There is not a lot of fun in making an amazing discovery and then realizing you are all alone. It is like the golfer who gets a hole-in-one with no one there to see it. As you look at involving others, ask these questions:

   • How can my students be involved in my learning?

   • How can family and friends get involved?

   • Can I involve other teachers?

5. **Game Time!** Games make teaching and learning fun. From the spelling bee of old to the computer math games of today, games play a significant role in student development. Teaching with Technology opens a new world of game options for today's teacher. Software technologists and entrepreneurs are busily developing interactive computer games to help students learn. Serious games are already used to train soldiers, pilots, firefighters, and police. In our grade 6 classroom, we use games to review lessons, practice literacy and numeracy skills, get exercise, and to break up lessons. To check out some of these fun classroom games, sign up for our newsletter and visit MrKent.net.

Step 6:

KEEP UP TO DATE

"Thanks, but I'd rather get my
financial advice off the Internet."

There is one common factor with technology. Change! As soon as you figure something out, it changes. As you learn how to use a new digital tool, the creator is busily improving it. Elsewhere a competitor of the product you have is making their product better, rendering the one you are adjusting to obsolete. So what do you do about it, scream a lot? I have done that. It does not help. The solution: stay up to date on changes with daily activities.

12 WAYS TO KEEP UP TO DATE

1. **Get involved.** Want to become familiar with changes in technology? Find a teaching technology community. Find out who knows about technology and become part of their learning group.

2. **Get on lists.** Every day e-newsletters keep people up to date on changes in education technology. Find the sources of these and get included.

3. **Be first in line.** Look for opportunities around you to be first in line to try a new technology.

4. **Contribute.** If your school has a website or a newsletter, become involved with keeping it current. Usually the individual responsible is on the lookout for items. This individual is "in the know" about changing and updating technology. Become his or her associate and ask to be included on informative releases.

5. **Find a consultant.** Most schools have access to designated technology consultants knowledgeable about Teaching with Technology. Get time with them and learn as much as you can about board policy and standards on Teaching with Technology.

6. **Daily e-learning.** One of the reasons we created a monthly newsletter, *MrKent.net News,* was to provide teachers with up-to-date information about technology and its impact on teachers. Subscribe at MrKent.net.

7. **Find a mentor.** When learning a new skill, have a mentor available to listen to questions (no matter how simple). Find an experienced colleague in your school using technology in his or her classroom. Ask to meet with that person to discuss integrating teaching with technology. As colleagues use technology, more opportunities will arise to share ideas and tips.

8. **Attend seminars.** There are a number of seminars, conferences, and professional development opportunities available to assist teachers in integrating technology into classrooms. Ask the following questions to make sure the seminar will be beneficial:

    •   Will there be hands-on training?

    •   Will technology be available in the seminar?

    •   Will the instructor be experienced in teaching with technology?

    •   Will the instructor be available for follow-up questions after the seminar or online in the days and months ahead?

    •   Are the seminar notes available on the Web for follow up?

9. **Talk to a manufacturer or distributor.** Providers of technology want you to be successful when using their products. Ask them for help, test drive their tools, attend one of their seminars, or email them with questions and concerns. Ask for assistance. If that does not work, ask again!

10. **Join an organization.** When looking for assistance with Teaching with Technology, I searched online and found an organization in Ontario, Canada. They provided a forum for teachers using technology. This organization, ECOO (Educational Computing Organization of Ontario, http://www.ecoo.org), has been a significant help in my development. They provided forums to learn, exposed me to like-minded teachers, and allowed me to share discoveries with others. Organizations like ECOO are emerging around the world. Seek out one close to you. Ask these questions to make sure the educational technology organization is right for you:

    •   What resources are available through the group?

    •   What are costs and time requirements?

    •   What teachers in your school or community are members?

    •   Can you attend a meeting without joining, to try it out?

    •   What communications (e.g., newsletters and magazines) are available?

11. **Read, listen, and watch.** Newspapers, blogs, newsgroups, podcasts, and videos are available for educators wanting to know more about teaching with technology. Major newspapers have technology/education sections, and

there are many websites like MrKent.net dedicated to educational technology. These resources are a treasure trove of information about new and changing technology. For example, in the printed newspaper I read today (the Canadian *National Post*), there was a fascinating article about the website Second Life. This interactive website takes you into a virtual world and holds fascinating possibilities for teaching in the future. Articles like these are thought provoking and spark conversations with other teachers and students.

12. **Commit to lifelong learning.** The best way for teachers to keep up to date is to commit to lifelong learning. Students are born into this ever-changing world and must continually adapt in order to succeed. If we are to facilitate their learning, we too must constantly learn and adapt.

• Commit in writing to your organization to be a lifelong learner. Ask them to help.

• Set learning objectives each quarter and year. Make a list of things you want to learn about, and outline how and when you will do this.

Items to learn	How I will learn	When I will do it
Second Life website	Research and try the website	March 15–18, 2008

• Keep an open mind about everything new in the technological world. Remember, the crazy science fiction idea of today may become your teaching tool of tomorrow.

THE FUTURE

"The human race is still evolving. Your baby was
born with extra thumbs for text messaging."

As educators, we have a mission to prepare students for the future—but do we actually do this? For future success, students must be able to do the following:

- Learn and adapt quickly to new software and hardware

- Navigate and create electronic content

- Confidently handle and compose emails

- Participate in online conferences and forums

- Use instant messaging with proper etiquette

- Troubleshoot technical problems

Educators, school administrators, political leaders, the business community, and parents need to work together to unleash the potential the virtual education community has to offer. They can do this by embracing technology more fully, closely monitoring the impact on student development, and investing in technology and training for the future.

TEACHING WITH TECHNOLOGY HEADLINES OF TOMORROW

Education will be different in the future than it is today. Here are some Teaching with Technology headlines of the future.

"Research Supports Teaching with Technology"

Research data now shows properly executed Teaching with Technology significantly improves student development.

"Teaching with Technology Is a Required Skill"

Teacher colleges include technology teaching in the new curriculum. Teaching with Technology is required for all front-line teachers.

"Technology Costs Drop"

The price of educational technology continues to decrease. More and more schools begin to add technology to their programs.

"The Essential Learning Tool"

Schools today have adopted personal learning devices for all students and teachers. Individuals in the business world have been utilizing the power of personal computing tools for many years. These devices are now serving as personal learning devices for every member of the school community.

"One Computer per Child"

Low-cost laptops are now used by children all over the world. These laptops are built to withstand harsh living conditions. The computers have long-life batteries, can be recharged manually, and have powerful wireless capabilities to enable students to access the Internet in remote regions.

"E-Textbooks Are Here"

Schools now pay a subscription to obtain online textbooks of their choice. This allows students unlimited access to up-to-date books. The financial burden printed books previously placed on our education system was staggering. Textbooks purchased every couple of years were replaced with a costly new book, not unlike the previous one.

"The Teacher on the Other Side of the World"

Teachers have access to thousands of approved experts from around the globe and utilize their expertise when teaching specific topics. Students ask questions via conferencing and witness live experiments and global events.

"The Virtual Field Trip"

Virtual worlds make it possible to create your own digital self (avatar) to travel and experience the world of cyberspace. Teachers take class field trips to the Amazon or the Great Barrier Reef within cyberspace.

"Instant Student Assessment"

With the use of laptops and handhelds, all teachers now record assessments of students instantly and open these assessments to interested secure parties such as the student, parents, other teachers, and administrators.

"Customized Learning"

Departments of education are now streamlining educational data such as marks, reading levels, medical history, achievements, learning disabilities, and attendance. This helps educators assess individual students and then customize individual lessons.

"Global Student Project Assigned"

Today, the first global student project was assigned by the United Nations. Worldwide collaboration has students from around the globe communicating with each other.

Yes, future possibilities in the global schoolhouse are mind boggling. Students studying about Africa teleconference with a classroom of children in Botswana. A student writing an essay on the holocaust has an instant message conversation with a holocaust survivor. An art lesson on Picasso begins with a question-and-answer period with his granddaughter.

The lone teacher in my grandparents' one-room schoolhouse would be amazed at these developments and proud of our accomplishments.

FUTURE SCHOOL DESIGN

Our current school buildings are designed without consideration for education technology. Governments and schools boards must consider changes. Here are some suggestions.

High-speed wireless Internet. High-speed wireless Internet access is critical for students and teachers. They need to be able to trust that their Internet connection will not slow down the learning process.

Built-in digital whiteboards. New classrooms need built-in digital whiteboards. This will avoid having to re-design the room later to accommodate the digital whiteboard.

Technology storage. Each student and teacher will be using a laptop in the near future. New and remodelled classrooms must be designed with storage areas for equipment.

Lighting, and sound. When using technology, lighting, and sound become important. Classrooms using technology need to make the learning experience as comfortable as possible. Poor speakers or a fuzzy screen can make learning difficult for students.

Pre-wired schools. Wiring is awkward in schools not designed with technology in mind. Buildings must have projectors and digital whiteboards securely mounted and conveniently wired.

Classroom pods. Some schools are not yet able to purchase digital whiteboards, laptops, and projectors for every classroom. Until they can, new schools need to build classrooms in pods, allowing groups of teachers to share technologies.

Current classrooms were designed for yesterday's tools. Today's classrooms must be created for or adapted to existing and incoming technological teaching aids. School boards, principals and teachers must start, "thinking outside the box and blackboard" to maximize the effectiveness of this new learning environment, including lighting, sound, storage, wiring, security and interactivity
    In the following graphic, Promethean provides just one example of a new technology-adapted classroom layout.

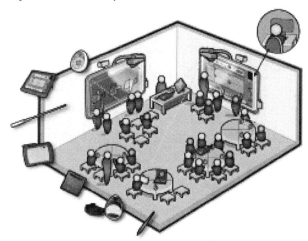

Future Promethean ActivClassroom

STANDARDS AND BEST PRACTICES

The use of technology for teaching in classrooms around the world is increasing daily. In addition to studies on the effectiveness of technology delivery in student development, documented standards, recommendations, guidelines, and best practices are required for teachers, principals, students, staff, and parents. Subjects include the following:

- Use of technology, security, and confidentiality standards

- Student, teacher, staff, and parental responsibilities for using technology

- Communication standards and etiquette

- Teacher technology skill requirements and training standards

- Lesson development and classroom implementation standards and best practices

- Hardware and software, purchasing, and maintenance standards

- Student use of technology, skill requirements

Many departments and boards of education have developed their own technology standards and best practices. Before creating your own, do some research to make sure your standards and best practices are thorough.

IF I COULD DO IT ALL OVER AGAIN

Have you ever wanted to do something again to avoid mistakes? Here, for your benefit, is my confessional. If I could implement technology over again, this is what I would do.

Make a Better Plan

When beginning to build virtual education communities, I had a rough plan in mind. Make a detailed written action plan and revisit it often.

Visit More Schools

I visited a few schools using technology, but I now realize there are many different ways to build a virtual education community. Visit a wide range of educational institutions, including private schools, public schools, colleges, and universities and use their best features.

Talk to Teachers Using Technology

There is nothing better than talking to someone who has gone through the same experience. Speak to educators who are building technology into their classrooms to obtain practical advice and avoid potential problems.

Use a Guide

When I started, there were no instruction manuals to help me reach my goals. Today there are many great books to help educators integrate technology into their classrooms.

Attend More Ed-Tech Conferences

Educational technology conferences were beneficial and informative. Many of my ideas came from these conferences. Attend these conferences and review their content to learn how others are teaching with technology.

Test Drive Products

Most people test drive a vehicle before they purchase it. Educators must test drive educational technology hardware, software, and websites before they use them in their classrooms. Compare and test products to make sure you are getting the best product at the best price.

CONCLUSION

When you start a book with an introduction, you should have a conclusion. Perhaps with a subject like Teaching with Technology, there is no conclusion. It is a never-ending work in progress. As this book was written over the summer and fall of 2007, we witnessed a number of significant changes in the hardware used to deliver technology and the software used to organize and shape it.

If you are a teacher who is considering using technology in the classroom, I encourage you to take the plunge by following the 6 steps. Will it be worth it? Over the last six years, I have experienced the joy and excitement of teaching using these new technological tools. My students adapted quickly and drove more changes with their interest and enthusiasm.

Some school leaders are sceptical on technology's effect on learning. What do you think? Will technology be the way of the future in our classrooms or a passing phase? Perhaps the Christmas flyer in today's mail is prophetic—the headlines are "Toys for Tech Savvy Tots" and "Help Pre-schoolers Learn with Electronic Gifts."

Here come the tech-savvy tots! Are you ready?

Lucas Kent
Victoria Harbour, Ontario, Canada
Jan 15, 2008

"Computers are incredibly fast, accurate and stupid; humans are incredibly slow, inaccurate and brilliant; together they are powerful beyond imagination."

—Albert Einstein

Appendix A

Know the Web

Good e-learning relies on quality websites. With the millions of sites, it is sometimes difficult for educators to make informed decisions. To help you in this challenge, here are MrKent.Net's current *Top 40 Websites for Teachers*. This is a small sample of the websites available to you on the Internet and must be added to, replaced, and tested constantly to ensure the links are current and effective. This list is updated on a regular basis and is available on our website MrKent.Net.

E-Learning

Promethean Planet—http://www.prometheanplanet.com
When you subscribe for free at Promethean Planet you will have a vast range of digital whiteboard resources at your fingertips.

BrainPOP—http://www.brainpop.com
BrainPOP has hundreds of short animated movies and quizzes on various subjects. Try a free trial or purchase the subscription that suits you.

Edutopia—http://www.edutopia.org
The George Lucas Foundation created this site to inspire innovative teaching. As a bonus, you can subscribe to their free magazine, *Edutopia*.

SchoolTube—http://www.schooltube.com
This website allows educators to share approved videos nationwide, empower students and encourage creativity.

eSchool News—http://www.eschoolnews.com
eSchool News covers education technology in all its aspects, from legislation and litigation, to case studies, to purchasing practices and new products.

BBC Schools—http://www.bbc.co.uk/schools
An outstanding, interactive, and information website for educators and students. The site contains activities, games, videos, and lessons for every grade level.

Woodlands Junior School Kent—http://www.woodlands-junior. kent.sch.uk
A world famous school website that has thousands of interactive activities.

Discovery School—http://school.discoveryeducation.com
A site every educator should put in his or her favourites folder. This site is filled with information, videos, lesson plans, puzzle makers, clipart, teaching tips, and much more.

Scholastic.com—http://www.scholastic.com
Scholastic has something for teachers, students, parents, administrators, and librarians. The site is overflowing with lessons, stories, tips, activities, and more.

IKnowThat—http://www.iknowthat.com.com
This site has games and activities for every subject area. There is also a virtual beehive that allows students to participate in a safe virtual world.

Funbrain—http://www.funbrain.com
This site has educational activities and just plain fun games for kids.

Fun School—http://funschool.kaboose.com
Fun School is a student favourite, filled with educational games and activities.

Math

Virtual Manipulatives—http://nlvm.usu.edu/en/nav/index.html
The National Library of Virtual Manipulatives is a great addition to an educator's arsenal. The site contains hundreds of interactive Web-based manipulatives.

Learning Clip—http://www.learningclip.co.uk
Learning Clip has entertaining math video clips and interactive activities to incorporate into lessons.

Create a Graph—http://nces.ed.gov/nceskids/createagraph/default.aspx
This great website helps students create and manipulate graphs quickly.

Interactivate—http://www.learningclip.co.uk
Interactivate has hundreds of Java-based lessons, a dictionary of math terms and lessons for teachers and students.

Math Playground— http://www.mathplayground.com
Math Playground helps elementary and middle school students practice their math skills.

Language

Spelling City—http://www.spellingcity.com
This is a great website for practicing spelling. Students and teachers can customize spelling lists and review words in fun ways.

Big Universe—http://www.biguniverse.com
Big Universe has an extensive collection of picture books for students and teachers. Browse their free collection, personalize your bookshelf, and even create your own picture book.

Lookybook—http://www.lookybook.com
Lookybook makes it possible to view entire picture books from cover to back on a digital whiteboard.

Dance Mat Typing—http://www.bbc.co.uk/schools/typing
BBC's Dance Mat Typing is a great free online program that teaches students the basics of typing in a fun and competitive way.

Poetry Teachers— http://www.poetryteachers.com
Poetry Teachers helps you inspire a love of poetry in your students and teach kids how to write different types of poems.

Science & Health

National Geographic—http://www.nationalgeographic.com
National Geographic's website is as rich and informative as their magazines. Their live cameras, videos, vivid pictures, and games inspire students to learn about our amazing planet.

Wonderville—http://www.wonderville.ca
Surf around the interactive world of Wonderville and discover some interesting things about the world around.

ElectroCity—http://www.electrocity.co.nz
ElectroCity is an online computer game that lets players manage their own virtual towns and cities. It's great fun to play and also teaches students about energy, sustainability and environmental management.

The Wild Classroom—http://www.thewildclassroom.com
Wild Classroom is a non-profit organization whose goal is to provide educators with high quality science/biology videos to use in their classrooms.

The Yuckiest Site— http://yucky.discovery.com
Discovery Kids teaches students all about the gross and disgusting stuff around and inside us.

Kids Health—http://kidshealth.org
An informational website to help kids and teens learn about health issues.

Social Studies

CNN Student News—http://www.cnn.com/studentnews
CNN Student News is a free daily news program designed for students. The site also provides teachers with daily lessons, activities, and quizzes.

History Detectives Kids—http://pbskids.org/historydetectives
PBS History Detectives Kids has video clips, games and tips to help students learn about history.

CBC Archives for Teachers—http://archives.cbc.ca/for_teachers
CBC has compiled news footage of the past and added great resources for teachers.

The Arts

National Gallery of Art—http://www.nga.gov/kids/kids.htm
NGA is a great website with amazing tools for K-8 students to practice their art skills.

Kerpoof—http://www.nga.gov/kids/kids.htm
Kerpoof is a website designed by Walt Disney where students create original artwork, animated movies, stories and much more. There are also ideas and lesson plans for educators to use.

Sphinx Kids—http://www.sphinxkids.org
This site teaches students about classical music using games and interactive activities.

Media & Safety

Understand Media—http://www.understandmedia.com
Understand Media provides free resources to help teachers help kids learn the importance of understanding media. They offer free articles, lesson plans, podcasts, a blog, videos, and much more.

Values.com— http://www.values.com
Values.com is a great website to use to teach character education and media literacy.

Plugged In—http://www.pluggedinonline.com
Plugged In reviews music, TV shows, and movies to help teachers and parents make informed choices about what their children are exposed to.

Net Smartz—http://www.netsmartz.org
Net Smartz is an Internet safety site, with crucial information for kids, teens, parents, educators, and law enforcement. The site has videos, stories, and games to educate about online safety.

ChildNet—http://www.childnet-int.org
This nonprofit organization is working on many projects to help children use the Internet in positive ways. The site also contains practical tips for parents about the dangers of the Internet.

Kim Komando—http://www.komando.com
Finding it hard to keep up with the changes in technology? Kim Komando simplifies the process for you with her practical computer tips and advice.

APPENDIX B

Start with a Plan

A good lesson plan is an essential tool for educators. When creating a lesson, Today's teacher needs to consider utilizing technology in their teaching and if appropriate build it strategically into their planning.

This lesson plan template was developed by John Migliore from Lawfield Elementary School in Hamilton, Ontario. I like this lesson because of its use of technology and commitment to differentiated learning. This lesson and others are available on our website MrKent.Net.

Differentiated Instruction and *The Outsiders*
By John Migliore, Lawfield Elementary School

Is there anything more tried and true than the impact of *The Outsiders* by S.E. Hinton on intermediate students? Differentiated instruction is a great way to add a new dimension to this old favourite.

Instructional Strategies
Instructional strategies will include:
- Setting objectives.
- Providing feedback.
- Providing recognition.
- Non-linguistic representation.
- Cooperative learning.

Technology Categories
Technology usage will include:
- Multimedia presentations.
- Communication software.

Teacher-Directed Learning Activities
Teacher will:

- Read portions or even the entire novel aloud.

- Provide materials necessary for each of the following activities.

- Serve as a guide-on-the-side for student-directed learning activities.

Student-Directed Learning Activities
Student-directed learning activities will fall into six possible groupings. These groups should be formed based on student interest.

The group activities include:

1. **Sing Your Heart Out** – Write a song about one of the characters in *The Outsiders*. Include as many character traits and significant events as possible. The song should be no less than 200 words. Once the song is written, create music to go with it, using Acoustica Mixcraft 4 or Garage Band. You will be presenting the song and music in class.

2. **Create an Abstract Image** – Create an abstract image with pastels and crayons that uses only line, shape and colour to represent a character from *The Outsiders*. You will be presenting your work in front of the class and explaining the reasoning behind your artistic choices.

3. **Stage a Character Debate** – Who is more of a criminal: Johnny Cade or Dallas Winston? Group members must take opposing sides and prepare the defense of their character... and the fall of the other character. Be prepared to stage your argument in front of the class.

4. **Create an Interactive White Board Game** – Use phrases from *The Outsiders* to create an interactive word guess game that reviews the characteristics of the main players. Be prepared to stage the game with the entire class.

5. **Choreograph a Rumble** – Watch video clips from various productions of *West Side Story*. Stage the rumble that appears in chapter 9 of *The Outsiders*. Focus on bringing in elements from the novel and turn those elements into a choreographed dance. You should consider a number of ways to safely dramatize the events.

6. **Dramatize a Scene from The Outsiders** – Choose a scene from *The Outsiders* and prepare a dramatic presentation. You may have to add to the scene to create enough dialogue for your presentation, which will be roughly 3 to 5 minutes in length. You may also choose to assign a narrator.

Differentiation – Accommodations
- Enable a high level of student interest.
- Activities require a varying level of reading, writing and/or oral ability.

Differentiation – Extensions
- Create a CD that includes your song and album cover art.
- Create a virtual gallery of your abstract art using digital photos of your work in a slide presentation set to music.
- Share your game with another class also studying *The Outsiders*.
- Stage presentations at an assembly or digitally record your performances to be viewed at a later date.

Closure – Reflection
- Arts festival to celebrate and display what the students have created.
- Student comment sheet for feedback.

Glossary

Assistive technology. Technology that assists students to perform regular educational tasks.

Avatar. An online digital character used in virtual worlds.

Blackberry. Digital handheld device that allows you to make phone calls, send emails and text messages, and surf the Internet.

Blog. An online journal that expresses insight, opinion, and expertise on various subjects.

Blogger. Online blogging program that helps you write, post, and view blogs.

BrainPOP. Website that contains short educational videos, featuring cartoon characters Tim and Moby.

CD-ROM. Read-only CDs that are used to distribute computer software.

Cloze. Exercises or assessments that consist of a portion of text with words removed. Students are then asked to replace the missing words.

Content-control software (censorware, Web-filtering software). Software that controls the content students are permitted to view on the Internet.

Course management software. Software, such as Moodle, that helps educators build online learning communities.

Cyberspace. A term used to describe the digital world of the Internet and computing devices.

Desktop. Personal computer that every student has access to, either at home or in the school computer lab.

Digital camera. Cameras that do not require film or developing. Digital cameras allow the photographer to download pictures to various devices for viewing and printing.

Digital slate (digital tablet). A hardware device that allows individuals to interact with a digital whiteboard without standing in front of the board.

Digital whiteboard (interactive whiteboard). Whiteboards that have digital images projected on them by digital projectors. Digital whiteboards allow teachers and students to interact with the digital images projected on the board.

Differentiated instruction. A style of teaching to various levels of abilities.

Email. A form of communication via the Internet that allows individuals to send text, graphics, video, and computer files to each other.

E-zine. An online newsletter, which allows individuals to subscribe, similar to a magazine.

Flash drive. A small device that is inserted into USB ports and allows individuals to save files from their computer onto it.

Forums. Online discussion groups where individuals can post their own opinions and respond to views on various topics.

Google. The famous search engine that scans the Web to find sites that are related to your search terms.

Handheld (PDA). Small, portable computer that allows teachers to assess students anywhere throughout the school day.

Hardware. Physical digital devices, such as digital whiteboards, laptops, and student-response systems.

Hot Potatoes. A free software program that allows teachers to create digital activities and tests, which they can then upload to their online communities.

Instant messaging. Sending a digital text message to another individual over the Internet.

Internet. A worldwide connection of computer networks that transmit data.

iPod. A portable device, created by the company Apple, which stores and plays music and digital files.

Laptop. Portable personal computer that gives teachers the mobility they need to plan and teach effectively.

Moodle. An open-source software program that helps schools create an online community with customized features.

MP3. A portable device that allows an individual to save and play music or digital files.

Online learning community. An interactive website that allows teachers, students, and parents to communicate and learn using the Internet.

Open source. Free software that is created and enhanced by groups of individuals connected through the Internet.

Peripherals. Devices that are add-ons to your main computing component (i.e. printer, mouse).

Podcasting. Creating and posting an audio file on the Internet; also, creating a "feed" so that individuals can subscribe and have the audio file automatically sent to their computer.

Printers. A device that allows you to print text and graphics from your computer onto paper.

Projectors (digital projectors). A projection device that attaches to your computing device and projects the image onto a screen, wall, or digital whiteboard.

Scanners. A device that allows individuals to scan hard copies of pictures and text and covert them to a digital file on a computing device.

Search engines. Sites, such as Google and Yahoo, that allow individuals to view websites that relate to the search term they enter.

Second Life. A virtual world where people create their own avatars and live in a virtual online community.

Short-throw projectors. Projectors that are attached to digital whiteboards and project a large image over a short distance.

Software. Computer applications that are loaded onto computers, which allow individuals to perform various tasks.

Spreadsheets. A computer program that allows individuals to add text and create formulas to help them track and calculate data.

Student-response systems (clickers). Tools that allow students to respond to questions simultaneously and anonymously. Student-response systems also allow teachers to collect assessment data quickly and efficiently through their computer.

Text message. A short text message commonly sent by a mobile phone or PDAs.

Video conferencing. Allows individuals to meet together digitally, speak to each other, and view each other on their respective computer screens.

Virtual education community (VEC). The digital educational community that collaborates, communicates, and educates.

Virtual field trip. Websites and applications that allow individuals to visit real-life sites via their computer.

Web 2.0. Web-based communities that promote creativity, collaboration, and sharing between Internet users.

Webcam. A camera that allows individuals to project live or recorded video onto the Internet.

Web page. A page on the Internet. May contain text, graphics, video, etc.

WebQuest. A lesson that requires students to use the World Wide Web to learn about a topic.

Website. A collection of Web pages on a similar topic.

Wiki. Collections of web pages that allow anyone to modify, add or remove content.

Wikipedia. A large online encyclopaedia with millions of articles.

WordPress. Online blogging program that helps you write, post, and view blogs.

World Wide Web (www). The system of websites available to those who have access to the Internet.

PROMETHEAN
ACTIVBOARD

INTERACTIVE WHITEBOARDS
~
TABLEAUX INTERACTIFS

ACTIVSLATE

ACTIVOTE

ACTIVEXPRESSION